Poems on th

A Book of Poetry by R

Publisher Richard Archer.

Editor Ruth Archer.

Year of Publication 2016.

Email: Richard.archer4@aol.co.uk

Website: Poems and More from Richard Archer

For further information please contact me at the above email.

ISBN: 978-1-326-73642-2

This book is dedicated to my wife and daughter, page 101 is for you.

I also dedicate this book to National Express West Midlands and their trusty bus route from Walsall to Birmingham. Without your comfy seats and reasonable travel time, a lot of poems in this book might never have been written.

Contents

Introduction

Poems on the Bus is the third collection of poetry from Walsall poet Richard Archer. Now in his fifth year of writing, performing and blogging about poetry, this book is a collection of another year of Richard's poems with the best of his website's work and brand new material.

This year has been a busy one for Richard with performances at festivals, open mics, literary events, appearing on TV, at libraries and more. In addition to all the performances Richard also found time to compile a book of the work of local poets from across the West Midlands. Entitled Diverse Verse the book is sold to support local charities. Richard has also worked with local film director Andy Simon on a collaboration for Andy's film "Jessica's Doll." The poem that forms the introduction to the film which they wrote together features in this book.

Also featuring in the book are the poems "Dinner for One," which was shortlisted in a competition by Theatre Cloud and "Machine Gun Poetry," and "Wooden Poetry," which were published by Black Napkin Press.

Online, Richard's poetry website "Poems and more from Richard Archer" celebrated its fifth birthday attracting visitors from all round the world and has hosted guest poets. His first book "Beer Froth" is now available on the Kindle.

Alongside all this Richard has written this his third book of poetry, "Poems on the Bus." The majority of the work found in this book was written on Richard's daily commute to Birmingham on the trusty 51 bus. In spite of adverse temperatures and early mornings poetry, seemed to thrive in this environment and from it this book was born.

Massive thanks to Andy Simon for his hard work on the book cover and design, huge thanks to Emma Dunn the cover model and big cheers to Aston Manor Road Transport Museum for allowing the cover to be shot there.

So why not hop on the poetry bus and see where it takes you!

Richard

Poems on the Bus

There's poetry everywhere you look,
Hiding in every cranny and every nook.
But you might be quite surprised,
If I told you I find it on a bus ride.

What you may see inside a bus or out,
Can spark poetry, have no doubt.
Take time to pause and think,
Look around what do you glimpse?

Views flashing by through the window,
Adverts for anything old and new.
Newspaper articles on faraway places.
The stories hidden in people's faces.

As the passengers and stops come and go,
Poems will start to take shape and flow.
Keep pen, paper or your phone near,
Write them down before they disappear.

Let an old familiar commute suddenly be,
Freshly filled with ideas and mystery.
You'll see poetry can be found by all,
Every bus journey you'll hear a poem's call.

Try it next time on a bus you travel,
Open your mind to what's around you.
You'll be pleasantly surprised,
When a poem appears before your eyes.

Poetry's the New Rock and Roll

Poetry's the new rock and roll,
Can't you feel it in your soul?
It's the new craze for boys and girls,
Poetry's going to take over the world.
Kardashians are yesterday's news,
It's poets people now choose.
They want words that aren't dumbed down,
Simon Cowell's had to leave town.
Now everyone has a goatee beard,
Even the girls which is cute not weird.
Everyone reads poetry all day,
"The world's rhyme crazy," the papers say.
Statues of poets are being raised,
Their birthdays are now holidays.
National Poetry day's all the time,
Kanye's now on the dole line.
Sadly as this poems speaks to you,
You know it's words aren't true.
You have a thought that leaves you cold,
Poetry really isn't the new rock and roll.
Although we know that we don't care,
Because our words we will still share.
Poetry may not be the new rock and roll,
But I prefer it if the truth be told.

My Darkish Desire

Every day I wake with the taste of you on my tongue
Which fuels my need to see you again.
As I rise I find
My resolve crumbles.
While my brain concocts feeble excuses
To cross your path today.

When we do meet
I'm happy to see you're ready.
You knew I would come.
Money changes hands, but our eyes don't meet.
I mumble my name, though you know it,
So never reply.

Your scent teases me
Helping me to wait, as I do every day.
I long to hold you.
To feel your warmth
Radiate through my hands.
Before our lips lock.

I sense you're ready.
I raise my eyes.
My heart skips
As my pulse accelerates.
Then I hear the words that make my day,
"Large mocha with sprinkles for Richard."

Jessica's Doll

This is a story about a little girl,
Jessica was her name.
She lived a carefree happy life,
Playing with dolls her favourite game.

But Jessica's happiness didn't last,
There came a very sad day.
When tragedy shattered her world,
As her parents suddenly passed away.

As Jessica had no one to care for her,
She was packed off to a children's home.
Where apart from a doll that had her name,
She was always on her own.

Jessica lived in the home until she was eighteen,
Then she was cruelly cast out.
Forced to beg for money on the streets,
All alone except for her doll she wandered about.

One day while begging a fierce storm broke
So Jessica sort escape from the rain.
To her surprise she stumbled on her old home,
So cautiously entered its doors again.

The old home was full of cobwebs,
Jessica explored as outside the wind cried.
Then as the thunder broke and crashed,
She got scared and ran to the cellar to hide.

There to Jessica's amazement she found,
An antique and very large chest.
Frightened she got inside and closed the lid,
She thought it was for the best.

To her horror Jessica found she was trapped,
The chest's lid had locked itself tight.
She lay in there for hours crying,
As the storm raged through the night.

Jessica screamed and screamed for help,
But nobody heard or was concerned.
She lay in the dark chest with just her doll,
As her childhood memories returned.

Jessica held her doll tightly and made a wish,
"I want to be a doll forever," she wept.
Then with that she stopped breathing,
Stopped aging and then she slept.

I'm Just a Lonely Goldfish.

In my precariously held plastic bag
I'm the new thing of which to brag.
As teenage mouths gape and drool
Because it appears I'm just so cool.
Luckily I make it home
Where for a while I'm proudly shown.
Then I'm left alone on a top shelf
Unable to ask for any help.
Only briefly novel, now I'm a chore
Hungry while my owner snores.
Maybe if I was a human child
The press would go wild.
But loneliness isn't my worse worry
As it seems I was named in a hurry.
And despite my owners justifying speeches
I don't understand why I'm named Peaches?

Brain Donor

I'm really worried about my brain,
As lately its use to me causes doubt.
So I popped in to see my Doctor,
Who told me it had to come out.

Unsurprisingly I stopped in my tracks,
Then said to the Doc, "how can you tell?
Plus I'd really like a second opinion."
"OK sir," he said "you're ugly as well."

The Doc explained, "if your brain's no use,
And about it you become a moaner.
Then a brain transplant patient applies,
And you become a brain donor."

So it's bye-bye to my cortex,
Farewell to my neurological mass.
Goodbye to my little grey cells,
I hope my brains loss will soon pass.

Now in between my ears,
Replacing what I had to discard.
Is a mobile phone ten quid special,
One gigabyte sim card.

So I find I never get upset,
I don't miss my brain, I'm not glum.
I smile and drool all day long,
Happily comfortably numb.

Nature vs. Numpty

I once read on the internet that Mount Everest,
Is an incredible eight thousand metres high.
I'm sure this towering monument inspires,
While challenging the bold to climb it.

No me though, I'm not that keen on climbing.
If I have to attempt a tame incline,
To reach a tempting ice-cream van.
I puff and pant into my ninety-nine and flake.

Anyway, I'm sure I read on the back of a matchbox,
That the Nile River is six million metres long.
I imagine this spectacle surging through the desert,
Teeming with aquatic fauna swimming it its waters.

I'm not really that keen on swimming.
Though if I'm pushed I can manage,
A couple of lengths of the local pool.
In a flailing doggy-paddle style.

A bloke down the pub once told me,
That a tortoise called Jonathan was
One hundred and eighty four years old.
Living a long and it seems happy tortoise life.

I'm fourty six years old, and not happy.
In fact I complain I have arthritis
If I am forced out of my easy chair
To walk to the local chip-shop.

It seems unlike me nature endures magnificently
Never complaining it just silently inspires.
So long after I am dead, buried and decomposed
Nature will simply and perfectly just carry on.

I think I like Pork Scratchings just a bit too Much

You are beauty to my eyes, a deep fried Venus de Milo,
They should hang you in the Tate, they'd make millions.
I can no longer resist you and reach out like a nervous lover,
Shakily pressing you to my lips, each kiss feeling like our first.

In my mouth you break like the splash of a frisky sea wave,
Your sodium tang threatens to drown my taste buds.
My teeth are the rocks on which you dash yourself,
As you drown I consume you body and soul with no regret.

Trying to Understand Love

Some search the internet for it,
Others have nothing but regret for it.
Anyone can lose their mind to it,
Sometimes you're just blind to it.
Prudes are not proud of it,
The perverse get aroused by it.
The grateful nourish a spark of it,
The lost grope in the dark for it.
Weddings are booked on it,
Lovers seem hooked on it.
Diamonds are bought for it,
Duels are fought for it.
People are thrilled by it,
Others are killed by it.
Computers try to scan it,
Religions try to ban it.
The bold travel the world for it,
The content don't care for it.
Some never want a part of it,
Others quietly lose their heart to it.
The hopeful look all around for it,
While many die having never found it.

The Lost Art of Queuing for the Bus

Many things have vanished in the mists of time
Books, plays, films and works of art sublime.
But recently vanishing without any fuss
Seems to have been the art of queuing for the bus.
Gone are the days when folk would stand in line
Politely getting on the bus one at a time.
Nowadays it seems it's quite impossible
To get on a bus without being pushed or jostled.
This madness starts before the bus has arrived
Passengers mingle suspiciously their plans devised
So when the bus arrives but before it thinks of stopping
They'll be first in the queue due to their nefarious plotting.
Some folks watch from afar while others lurk near
But they are all ready when the bus is here
To quickly form a mob around its door
Not caring who gets pushed to the floor.
Bags, trollies and brollies are widely used
To get their owners to the front of the queue.
Children old and young begin to cry
As desperate bus boarders push them to the side.
Old folk tut loudly but are ignored
As the eager stampede through the bus doors
Even though passengers are still trying to get off
For this mob that's no reason to stop.
It's almost as if someone has said
There's a prize for who gets on first, alive or dead.
I've seen better behaved rugby scrums
That would act more politely when a bus comes
And I wouldn't be surprised if one night
The bus queue erupted into a fight.
And those who are found standing last
Will be awarded a special bus pass
That allows them for all next month
To the front of the bus queue to jump
But I bet even after all this fuss
They still fight to be first on the bus.

If I Won the Lottery

A lot of people say if they won the lottery
That the money wouldn't change their life.
That they'd live as they always had,
In their suburban semi with their wife.
I say that's bull really
I know that if I won the lottery today.
Then overnight my life would change
In some very spectacular ways.

I'd bath every day in real ale
I'd wipe my bum on fifty pound notes.
I'd very rarely be found sober
I'd buy every copy of the books I wrote.
I'd eat platinum for breakfast
I'd scoff bullion for lunch.
I'd chew precious stones for tea
Then for a snack on silver nuggets I'd munch.

I'd buy a diamond encrusted back scratcher
I'd buy up all the Wetherspoons.
I'd buy a triffid for the garden
I'd buy a house on the moon.
I'd buy a robot butler and coffee machine
I'd buy the bat cave and in it I'd hide.
I'd buy android body guards
I'd buy mines for my drive outside.

Then when I'm older I'll refuse to behave
In my panda skin dressing gown.
I'll commission marble statues of myself
To deface the streets of my home town.
And when I finally kick the bucket
Spare no expense when I expire.
I want a funeral with all the trimmings
I don't want to be seen off by just a choir.

I want a jewel encrusted gravestone
To proclaim where I rest
Here lies the UK's former richest man
Who passed away doing his utmost best.
Too die and spend all his money
So his funeral went unpaid
And now his worn out body lies
On the local tip in a shallow grave.

Creation

In the beginning there was the word,
Waiting patiently to be written down.
Luckily there was also a poet with a pen,
Who imagined he could easily capture the word,
Then tame it over seven days
On to a piece of paper.

On the first day the poet happily picked up his pen and eagerly began to write.
On the second day the poet reluctantly crossed out what he'd written.
On the third day the poet studied the paper then angrily screwed it up.
On the fourth day the poet unscrewed the paper and doggedly wrote some more.
On the fifth day the poet read what he'd written and swore to quit poetry.
On the sixth day the poet forced himself to rewrite everything he'd already put down.

On the seventh day the poet picked up the tattered piece of paper
Then he screwed his A4 world into a near perfect ball.
Taking aim he pitched his creation with practiced accuracy
In to his overflowing bin.
Then he put down his pen, went to the pub and rested.
This was good.

Beardy Weirdy at the Symphony Hall

As I prop up the overpriced bar
Waiting to enjoy the concert.
From near and from afar
I can hear the whispering start.
"Oooh look at him he's got tattoos
Oooh look he's got a shaved head.
Oooh look trainers not shoes
He looks like he's just got out of bed!
Oooh look at his unshaven face
Oooh look at his scruffy beard.
Oooh is he in the right place?
He really just looks weird.
I'm sure he's carrying a gun
What's that, is it a bomb?
He's a convict on the run
Call the Police someone!"
After I explain to the Security man
I'm really here for the show.
That I really am a classical fan
He reluctantly lets me go.
I start to think and give myself a review
Should I have had a shave?
Should I have covered my tattoos?
So folk weren't scared into an early grave.
I can't decide but I know who my detractors are
So I hide in the nearest car park.
Then as those stirrers return to their cars
I leap out and scare them in the dark
Shouting, "yes I'm a beardy weirdy,
Of that I certainly cannot lie.
And I'm proud to be a beardy weirdy.
Until the day I die.
I'll write that on my grave I'm a weirdy
I'm going to put it on a new tattoo.
I'll always be proud to be a beardy weirdy
It's all thanks to you!

The Hedge Fund Manager who Secretly Wanted to be a Poet

Everyday to work on the tube he commutes,
Travelling the old familiar city routes.
Pretending to study his Financial Times
Furtively reading a poetry book hidden inside.

Then when he reaches his hedge fund firm,
His thoughts from poetry are forced to turn.
As he sits at his desk, his blood runs cold,
He can feel money clawing at his soul.

He begins to manoeuvre his clients cash,
Imagining instead ink on paper splash.
As he analyses charts of stocks and shares,
Only he knows it's rhyme for which he really cares.

His old school teachers are the ones he blames,
They always said exactly the same.
"Writing poetry won't earn you a living,
Stocks and shares are where you'll make a killing."

So his hedge fund he daily trims,
Dreaming of being able to make words spin.
Or writing rhymes applauded by all,
Instead of being a slave to Mammon's call.

Everyday back home on the tube he commutes,
Travelling the old familiar rural routes.
Staring at his crumpled Financial Times
Daring himself to take out the poetry book inside.

Chain Reaction

My neurons start to fire up,
Then they crash and spark.
In my head a chain reaction
Is threatening to start.

Words spiral around my brain,
Then ideas start to form.
This chain reaction's building,
To a cerebral storm.

I quickly grab a pen,
As ideas rapidly start to flow.
This chain reaction
Might make my head explode.

Ink stains my tongue and fingers
My knuckles turn white.
This chain reaction
Is gripping me tight.

My pen shatters,
Then neurons stop their flow.
Finally the chain reaction
Begins to slow.

Exhausted I finish
Unable to write.
But wary a chain reaction
Can return day or night.

Smoker's Blues

I remember when you could smoke on the bus
Lighting up on the deck upstairs.
It never caused any fuss
As even the driver smoked so didn't care.

I remember when you could smoke in the pub
Lighting up with your mates.
Ash trays full of cigarette stubs
Non-smokers each night had to fumigate.

I remember when you could smoke in the cinema
Smokers on the right, rest of you on the left.
Lighting up created no hysteria
As your nicotine clouds looked like special effects.

I remember when you could smoke at home
The simple pleasure of smoking anywhere.
Now we crouch outside with porcelain gnomes
Exiles in our own home but no one cares.

I Think my Sports Gene is Missing

My medical results came the other day
They were a sorry sight to bchold.
The Doctor looked at me and sighed,
"Son you might not live to be old.
Your cholesterol is high,
Your blood pressure is low,
Your heartbeat erratic,
And your pulse quite slow.
You need to start taking exercise,
Perhaps try a sport as a hobby?"
"Doctor, "I said, "that's not possible,
Sport's really not my cup of tea.
Just look closely at my results Doc
Give me some advice."
The Doctor re-scanned my paperwork
His eyebrows began to rise.
"It can't be, it's impossible," he spluttered,
"But your sport gene has withered and died.
I really must confirm these results,
What do you think about sport, which have you tried?"
"Well Doc, I didn't get a kick out of football,
Why people play cricket I'm stumped.
Tennis to me is just a racket,
I even get tired playing top trumps.
I've certainly never tried rugby,
Darts just seems pointless.
Swimming makes my heart sink,
Even thinking about sport gives me stress!"
"My dear boy you must try something,"
The Doc said. "You can't just sit and mope,
There must be some sport or activity you like.
Something with which even you can cope?"
"Well, "I said, "I enjoy a short walk to the pub Doc,
Where I might jump the queue at the bar.
Then I'll give my pint arm a workout,
But I don't like to take things too far!"
I think this upset the Doctor
He said, "your future's not bright."
So I left his surgery quite sharpish,
Then popped into my local for a pint.

Escape

Cautiously I weave through the city's streets
Hoping to spot a gap in its defences.
An escape route to dodge the urban chaos.
But I'm not quick enough, I'm seen.

The city cleverly outmanoeuvres me.
Chain link fences rapidly spring up,
High Vis jacketed guards are deployed,
Eagerly readying diversion signs.

I consult my electronic map
Tapping a route from A to bus.
I peer down gloomy back streets,
Desperate to circumvent chain link.

The city easily foils me again.
It throws up chewed up concrete,
Piling it across my escape route
Forcing me again to adapt quickly.

Alternate routes are no-go zones.
As slow hulking diggers and drills
Blockade bus and cycle lanes,
Oblivious to the honking tailback.

Tightly hugging the shadows
I place my faith in my electronic map.
Its reassuring beeps and buzzes
Shepherds me through hell to my goal.

I see my target, the last bus
Just as it starts to depart.
I desperately fling out my arm
Hoping the driver is on my side.

I finally escape the chaos,
Driving into the sunset
A Hollywood happy ending.
Until I wake tomorrow.

The Walsall Hippo

Solitary concrete guardian of Walsall,
Unmoving in your eternal vigil.
Never sleeping day or night,
Uncaring what the elements throw at you.

Walsall's stone Mona Lisa,
Smiling enigmatically at passers-by.
Patiently posing for visitor selfies,
Never complaining about pigeons.

I sat on you when I was young,
Now I bring my child to sit on you.
Hoping in the future,
You will be here to repeat the tradition.

I'm Spartacus

It's certainly a well-known historic fact,
That before Spartacus was crucified.
He had a large group of good mates,
Always willing to stand by his side.

But what isn't really that well known,
And what historians can't explain.
Is that before his death old Spartacus
Regularly used his mates to take the blame.

This trickery often annoyed Spartacus' wife
Who would to her husband's mates lose out.
Never able to get him to clean or tidy up
She would fly into a rage and shout.

"Spartacus you dirty swine,
You've been sick in the toilet bowl."
"I'm Spartacus," his mates would respond
"We were all sick if the truth be told."

The next day Spartacus' wife raged,
"I can't believe you've forgot my birthday."
"I'm Spartacus," his mates would chant
"We'll all get you a card straight away."

Only the day after his wife again complained
"Spartacus it's time you mowed the lawn."
"I'm Spartacus," his mates replied
"We're on our way to the shed, consider it done."

Finally when Spartacus was caught
Then on a cross strung up.
He died annoyed he'd not used his mates
To get out of doing the washing up.

Next to him hung his wife
Who took a last look at the lazy sod.
Then died murmuring "that some folk
Will do anything to get out of walking the dog."

The Romans ignoring the couple's grief
Put a sign above Spartacus which states.
"Citizens this will be your fate if you try
To get out of your jobs by using your mates."

The Optimistic Ice Cream Man

As the cold wind snaps and lashes
While the driving rain cuts and splashes.
The optimistic ice cream man
Attempts to sell his wares as best as he can.
His van's tinny chimes trickle out
Against the wind, trying to announce.
"It doesn't matter what the weather is
Come to my van you hungry kids.
See," the ice cream man says, "if the truth's told
Ice cream can actually be eaten hot or cold.
True, eating it hot can be a mess
But you won't like the ice cream any less."
Still the cold wind lashes
Still the driving rain splashes.
So as the weather has him beat,
The optimistic ice cream man retreats.
He starts his engine and drives away
Perhaps to return on a sunnier day.

Poem for my Daughter at 18 Months Old.

I think about our future
As I wrestle you into your vest.
Will we be battling some more,
Or will I be allowed a short rest?

Maybe your octopus like wriggles.
That throw off the bed clothes.
Might turn into octopus twists of logic
Bringing us both to mental blows.

I want to be the cool father
The one your friends think is great.
The one who buys you beer
And lets you stop up late.

I won't say no to you getting a tattoo,
As I have three of my own.
And I know my heart will break for you
If that boy you met never phones.

So I think about our future
As I wrestle you into your vest.
As long as I spend it with you
I don't care if I never rest.

The Weight of Words

I'm carrying a poet's briefcase,
Its weight makes my arms drag.
Curious as to the contents I ask the poet,
"It contains poetry dear boy," he replies.
So now I know what words weigh,
And I never thought they would be a burden.
As carrying poetry makes my back ache,
And has me gasping for breath.
So I have an idea and stop,
What if I was to open the case?
What if I set free the poetry within?
Imagine the words floating away
Caught by everyone around.
Who suddenly find joy in them.
Then my burden would be eased
Everyone carrying part of it.
Because when it comes to poetry
Surely it's better to share?

A Poem Left in a Holiday Cottage Guestbook

We loved your cottage, it's really very quaint,
But we feel there's an improvement you need to do.
Because we think the cottage could be better,
If you put up some window blinds in the loo.

Underwhelmed at Stonehenge

"I thought it would be a lot bigger,"
Said the rather dismissive visitor.
As they put aside so quickly,
5000 years of ancient history.
And somewhere in an ancient barrow,
A deceased Neolithic fellow.
Begins to revolve oh so quickly
He causes the first earthquake in Salisbury's history.

Revisiting Southbourne

Despite it being thirty years or more
Since my feet last trod it.
The old path to the beach is still
Hardwired in to my brain.
I walk past trendy coffee shops
Flanked by tattoo parlours.
That used to be newsagents or
Woolworths, my pocket money havens.
Walking the path I spy darting squirrels,
Possible descendants of
Those I fed KP nuts to years ago.
As I carry on the air gains a familiar salt tang
Then the sea comes into view.
I continue to walk where years ago I once ran
Down to the familiar sand and waves.
The wind bites not that it bothered a younger me
Who would swim until he was nearly blue.
But now I shiver in my jacket and wonder
If the ice cream shop sells mochas.
I feel different
Even though the sea is still the same,
As is the beach, the ice cream and the cold weather.
Then I realise the only thing that has really changed,
Is that a small fearless boy who was
Always excited by life's simple pleasures,
And cared not for the weather or coffee
Has grown up and forgotten what it was like
To once have been fearless and care free.

Poets Don't Carry Cash

Poets don't carry cash,
Instead they carry words.

Words stuffed into pockets, mixed with fluff.
Words forced into wallets, alongside old receipts.
Words withdrawn from dusty old accounts.
Words gathered from faded ashtrays on windowsills.

Poets should be rich,
But they can be careless.

Because as they fumble for the right word,
They spill out like so much loose change.
Which rolls around the floor, unwilling to be caught,
Lost, until found and read by puzzled strangers.

Ask a poet and they will swear they have words on them,
But when they check they find nothing.
The words have tumbled into sofa like cracks of their minds,
There to gather dust along with other lost ideas.

A poet's words start promisingly sharp and crisp,
Until they are nibbled by literary moths.
So they become tatty and unrecognisable,
Unaccepted and unusable.

Anyway as I said,
Poets don't carry cash.
Instead they carry words.
Which in spite of all the trouble they have with them,
They love to spend freely.

Pub Cat

Pub cat
Arches back.
Looking sleek
Furry cheek.
Tail flicking
Lip licking.
Ears alert
Mouth purrs.
Feline plea
Fuss me.

Big Fat Drops of Rain

Big fat drops of rain,
Falling on my brolly again.
Then dripping on to my head,
Before trickling down my legs.

Big fat drops of rain,
Flowing quickly, blocking drains.
Drowning the underpass,
Causing floods in a flash.

Big fat drops of rain,
Signal summer's here again.
Downpours today and yesterday,
It seems the rain is here to stay.

The Best Poem in the World

I'm going to sit down and write the best poem in the world.
I've got paper.
I've got my favourite pen.
I've got a mug of coffee.
I've got cigarettes.
I've got time.

Yes I'm certainly going to write the best poem in the world.
I've got integrity.
I've got experience.
I've got confidence.
I've got patience.
I've got a rhyming dictionary.

But it's harder than I thought to write the best poem in the world.
I look at the paper.
I chew my favourite pen.
I sip at my mug of coffee.
I consider a cigarette.
I should have time.

But

I've got emails to send.
A cigarette that needs smoking.
Facebook gossip to catch up on.
An urgent nap that needs taking.
And a million other things to do.

So I'm going to sit down and write the best poem in the world.

Tomorrow.

The World's Shortest Movie

"Tell me your plans while I'm helpless."
The hero bravely said.
"Never you utter idiot," said the villain,
Then he shot the hero dead.

Hanging

I'm hanging by my fingertips to the edge of the world.
It wasn't something I was planning to be honest.
I suppose I was just being nosey
Investigating if the grass really was greener etc.
And now here I am
Hanging by my fingertips to the edge of the world.

I sneak a look at what lies below my feet
But I can only see an uncertain mist
Whipped by a wind that seems to whisper, "let go."
But can I?
Should I?
Why would I?

My fingertips are starting to ache
It's hard to hang on to the edge of the world.
But I find strength as I do so
As I'm holding on to the familiar
It maybe the edge of the world
But it's my edge and I don't want to let go.

The mist below me swirls melodramatically
Did I glimpse something beyond it?
What are my eyes drawn to down there?
If I fall will I fall forever? An eternity of regret?
I'm hanging by my fingertips to the edge of the world.
I might let go in a minute, if I'm brave enough.

Writer's Block

An empty page on my computer screen,
Waits to be filled with my ideas and dreams.
But they're stuck in my head spinning round,
So I can't get my ideas out and down.
But I just know if I could make words flow,
If I could spit this idea out now.
If I could take this tangled mess,
Then with just a simple keyboard press,
The words would shift and my dream.
Would slowly appear upon my screen,
Instead of vanishing every night.
It would all make sense and read right,
Then let the printing presses roar.
Around the globe let my words soar!
Somewhere in this big old world,
People would actually read my words.
Look up from the page and think,
That just summed up my life in ink.
But that solace will never be,
My words only like my company.
They refuse to come out and make sense,
Just tease me before they vanish.
So ends another creative dream,
With an empty page on my computer screen.

Monochrome World

In the wearisome monochrome world
Everything is shades of black and white.
Humankind has been tranquilised
People live out a clockwork life.

They quietly catch dull buses,
Waiting patiently in drizzling rain.
Uncomplaining of grey smog
As they linger for drab trains.

Two-tone uniform policemen
Sedately walk silent beats.
Making people's muted lives,
Safe on their dingy streets.

Battleship grey homogeneous children
Shuffle softly to granite schools.
They only speak in whispers,
Not one of them plays the fool.

Once the dreary sun sets
In this world of black and white.
People retire to boring bedrooms,
To embrace the hushed night.

They close tired grey eyes,
That with tears start to stream.
As every night in bright colour
They live vicariously in their dreams.

The Breakfast Table Massacre

You wouldn't believe I'm a killer,
As to look at me you'd never guess.
That I'm actually a ruthless maniac,
It's something I've got to confess.

You see my breakfast table every morning,
Is the scene of my many crimes.
It's where I commit my foul murders,
Among the gingham table cloth lines.

My anger starts when I see the packets,
Their happy coloured pictures rile me.
My hatred rises and rises,
And triggers my breakfast killing spree.

I start with the Shredded Wheat
I smother them in milk and then,
Press them down into the liquid,
Where they are never seen again.

I then turn on the Weetabix,
I like to cover them in sugar.
Then crush them into little bits,
So they're unrecognisable to their mothers.

Then I single out my cornflakes,
And flick them around the room.
My eager evil fingers,
Send them flying to their doom.

Rice Krispies are my least favourite,
With their snap, crackle and pop.
I break them in half slowly,
While they beg me to stop.

My Neighbours are getting worried,
As every day I scream with delight.
And shout "death to all cereal,"
So they called 999 the other night.

But when the Police arrive,
They find me with just a cup of tea.
You see they'll never get a conviction
As I've eaten the evidence you see.

So when my name is mentioned,
All breakfast stuff starts to shiver.
They're worried I'll pay them a visit,
Me, the ultimate cereal killer.

Serial Killer I Love You.

When we first met I thought you were weird,
But it turned out it seemed I had nothing to fear.
Because even though you're a serial killer I found out
That of your love for me you said I should never doubt.
Now as I look back on our years together,
I should never have worried that our love wouldn't last forever.
At first I found your life odd and I had to remember,
That I shouldn't interrupt you while you dismember.
And I shouldn't worry that you still have your mom's clothes,
Or that upstairs her body is starting to decompose.
I learnt to ignore murder reports on the radio,
While never questioning what you buried under the patio.
But I still get anxious when you go out to paint the town red,
I worry for you as I lie awake with your mom in bed.
Wishing that you and your axe were here beside me,
But knowing how important it is that you finish your killing spree.
However I do have doubts that your love for me has passed,
When I discovered you'd dug a large hole in the vegetable patch.
I wish I hadn't bought you that saw for your birthday,
As you look at me funnily when you sharpen it every day.
We can't part now I get on with your mom so well,
I've even managed to get used to her smell.
You know that I'm not someone of who you can casually dispose,
As who will wash the blood off the patio with the hose?
Who will everyday your knives and hammers oil?
Who will lie for you when the police call?
Our vows said clearly till death do us part,
So I hope you can find it in your heart.
To forget any thoughts of murdering me,
I mean who will grill your victims for your tea?
But you smile at me and it melts my doubts,
I feel I've got nothing to worry about.
You say that hole in the vegetable patch
Is just for a bothersome badger you need to catch.
So as the sky begins to darken,
You take me out to show me this into the garden.
As you walk behind me carrying your spade,
I wonder why I was ever afraid.

Let Love Flow

Together we pick the rose from among the weeds,
Then we both grasp the stem.
Smiling as our blood mingles
Watching it run away among the stones.
That is how they find us
Our pale white hands clasped around a bright red rose.

Summer in the Arboretum

The bottomless lake.
Home to the killer pike.
Long lost illuminations,
Riding on my bike.

Fireworks in the Grange,
Funfairs as well.
Peacocks in cages,
That freshly cut grass smell.

Feeding the ducks,
Avoiding the swans.
A 99 and a flake,
A summer quickly gone.

I Hate Fish

I really hate fish, they stink of decay.
A malodorous odour that hangs around.
The ghost of the smell of a fish
Contaminating my clothes and polluting my nose.
Even when I'm out fish find a way to annoy me.
In the supermarket they stare at me.
Their cold dead eyes seeming to say,
I died for you and you just ignore me.

It's a well-known fact that fish ruin chips.
You can fry a piece as much as you want.
You can smother it in crispy batter,
But you can't hide that it's still a fish.
Look at those fish with their trout pouts.
They think they're the epitome of cool.
They want to brag about their trendy omega oils.
News update fish, that's in tablets now.

Fish I think we will need to compromise.
If you can agree to stay in the sea.
They I will stay on the land,
And I'm sure we'll both get on fine.
But if for one minute you make like your ancestors.
And you feel the need to walk out of the water.
Then I demand the right to develop gills,
Before I devolve back in to the sea.

Dreams of a Stuffed Toy Dog

What do stuffed toy dogs dream about?
Do they imagine felt teeth softly gnawing on foam bones?
Perhaps they dream of padded paws sneaking up on stuffed toy cats?
Maybe their cotton tongue drools over brown corduroy sausages?
Or do they romp on patchwork fields before snoozing on woollen rugs?

It could be their dreams are of simpler things.
They might smile as they snooze thinking of,
Someone who always hugs them tightly like there is no tomorrow.
Or they might be dreaming of the happiness that comes from,
Gazing into the eyes of someone who unconditionally loves them.

Intangible

Are our thoughts just abstract concepts
Intangible until we write them down?

Then as we keenly press pen to paper to free them
As we bring them to life and make them tangible

Are they grateful that we are doing so?
Are they happy with this so called freedom?

Or do they feel they have traded their liberty
For ink-chains and parallel cell-bars?

Do they rail against this bondage?
Do they chafe at their paper prison?

Until we hear their impassioned pleas
Making us realise we have done wrong

Then we do what we should have always done.
We speak and free our thoughts from their A4 cells.

Releasing them into the air where happily they dart
Like spectres, intangible again and free.

Wooden Poetry

On a fifth anniversary it's traditional
To give a wooden gift.
So I have chosen for you
Wooden poetry.
Not solid dependable oak poetry.
This is Ikea poetry.
Poetry you need a screwdriver to put together,
Words that should come with instructions.
This is old-fashioned wooden jigsaw poetry,
Poetry found in the loft with pieces missing,
Words that don't form a picture
No matter how hard you stare.

This is poetry you can burn.
Release words from wooden embers.
Poetry that generates no heat,
But just turns quickly to ash.
Ash that as if on cue
Is blown away by the wind.
This is poetry you can throw in rivers
To be enjoyed as it floats away.
This is poetry that no matter how hard you try to be rid of
Your dog will always bring it back.
This is poetry you can save for Bonfire Night.
Rhymes roast as marshmallows toast.

Next year comes iron.
Poetry formed from blood and metal.
If I've finished my jigsaw.

What Happened?

"What happened to my stick insect dad?
What happened to little Sticky?"
"Well son.
Because he looked just like a stick
One day he gave me the slip.
And I in no way trod on him
Then hid his body in the bin."

"What happened to my cat dad?
What happened to dear old Fluffy?"
"Well son
Fluffy was feeling quite lonely so
To an old lady with lots of cats she had to go.
And I in no way caught her crapping in my slipper
Then sent her on a one way journey down the river."

"What happened to my dog dad?
What happened to trusty old Sandy?"
"Well son.
Sandy liked going outside to play
Sadly the gate was open so he got away.
And in no way did he with my leg get frisky
So I had to beat him down with a bottle of whiskey."

"What happened to mom dad?
What happened to my mom?"
"Well son
She's not well at the moment so
To the hospital she had to go.
I certainly didn't catch her in bed with a man from down the road
Then bury both their bodies under our patio.

"Now son if you too don't want to disappear
Then I suggest this conversation ends right here.
And I promise that if you go out on to the patio
You'll be closer to your mother than you'll ever know."

An Ode to my First Ever Star Wars Action Figure

I remember how keen my fingers were
To tear you quickly out of your box.
Then equip you with your trusty blaster,
Which up our hoover was soon lost.
Oh Star Wars Death Squad Commander
I loved you despite your lack of elbows and knees.
I was just happy to own a piece of Star Wars
In those days us kids were easy to please.
Sadly I couldn't afford the Death Star
To give you a base from which to command.
So from an old box the washer came in,
I armed myself with a black felt and a plan.
To transform that mountain of waste card,
Into what I thought for you was a fitting base.
Full of trap doors, exhaust ports and cell blocks,
Plus a hidden trash compactor space.
So when you adventured with Action Man,
Or fought off a LEGO rebel attack.
You defended your cardboard Empire with pride,
But now I find that as I write this and look back.
That I wonder if I'd left you in your packet,
And put you safely away in the loft
That today your eBay value,
Might have covered a plasma TV's cost.
But my young hands just wanted to play,
I couldn't keep you to myself.
Would we have had half as much fun
If I'd left you in the box on my shelf?

Famous on the Bus

Someone famous must be on my bus,
People look around and fuss.
I wonder who this celeb could be,
Are they sitting near to me?
Then I notice the CCTV,
Broadcasting for all to see.
My stubbled chin and thinning hair,
On the security screen up there.
I don't mind that people now see,
That I am slumped in my seat.
With my face tired and drawn,
As I barely conceal a yawn.
But what I really do regret,
Is that I'm not captured at my best.
I wished I looked more composed,
Not on CCTV picking my nose.

Twitter Time

I'm tweeting at the bus stop,
That I'm standing in the rain.
I'm tweeting on the bus
Throwing off my Luddite chains.
I'm tweeting as to walk to work,
Heedless of any danger.
I'm tweeting just after,
I bumped into a stranger.
I'm tweeting funny pictures,
Well they're funny to me.
I'm tweeting pure nonsense,
I'm the king of comedy.
I'm tweeting at my desk,
Ignoring my fellow workers.
I'm tweeting that my boss,
Has just collared me as a shirker.

Machine Gun Poetry

Poetry is a weapon that I always have ready.
My brain is fully loaded with verbal ammo,
My tongue is always keen to open fire,
I'm ever ready to deal out poetic justice.
I know my combat drill, let's do it.

I visualize my verse.
I ready my rhyme.
But most importantly,
Once I pick a target,
I don't recite until I see the whites of their eyes.

Then I never hesitate to unleash poetry,
I let slip my words of war,
Savouring the impact of each phrase fired,
I empty my verse into the target.
Watching them fall with a poem between the eyes.

As my mouth begins to smoke I halt,
Then I flick the safety catch on my couplets.
Pausing my performance,
But remaining vigilant,
Poetry is a weapon and I always shoot first.

I Think I'm Going Bald

I tentatively touch the back of my head
Trying to work out if my hair is still there.
I twist my neck as I look in the mirror
I can see a bald spot I swear.
Worried I consult recent family photos
Looking for ones of me shot from behind.
My head seemed to glare as the camera flashed
People look like they've been struck blind.
There's no doubt about it I'm going bald
Or optimistically my hair's now very thin.
I gaze at the mirror reflecting on the irony
That the hairiest part of my head's now my chin.

Let there be Light

Suddenly a voice spoke saying, “let there be light.”
And there was.
As an opening line you have to admit it was pretty damn good
We were expecting great things to follow.
But the light opened our eyes to all the things we didn’t want to see.
There was the litter blowing down the street,
All those depressing newspaper stories,
And the tired lines under everyone’s eyes.
You can’t deny light was needed and I don’t want to stand in the way of progress,
But we were hoping for something a little friendlier.
How about let there be rock, so I can play my air guitar,
Or what about let there be cake……mmmm cake.
But without light I suppose I might get a bit stuck,
How will I be able to play my air guitar if I can’t find it?
How will I be able to stuff my face with cake if I can’t see it?
So I phoned up light’s boss and we had a chat,
And we came to an agreement.
So the voice spoke again saying, “let there be light, in moderation,
And let it come with a dimmer switch so it can be adjusted to suit individual needs.”

The Secret Life of Pistachios

To sit down and attempt to write a poem about pistachios
Is really a lot harder than you might suppose.
As they're not that exciting, they just sit still and grow,
Only moving if the wind around them blows.
Because exciting things don't happen to pistachios you know.

No, never has a super villain with oily black moustachios,
Fiendishly hijacked the world's supply of pistachios.
Remaining unchallenged until a nut loving hero arose,
Who defeated the dastardly villain with some superb judo.
Because these things don't happen to pistachios you know.

At no point did macadamia lovers invent a crazy gizmo,
That would vaporise instantly every single pistachio.
Enabling their snack rival to be completely deposed,
So the world would have to eat only the nuts they chose.
Because nothing bizarre happens to pistachios you know.

The news has never broadcast that all pistachios,
Were accidentally to deadly radiation exposed.
Causing nut lovers to glow then fall like dominoes
Leaving their dead bodies in the streets to decompose.
Because pistachios aren't the stuff of sci-fi you know.

So I'm left with nothing interesting to write about pistachios,
Except to make up a lot of right nonsense I suppose.
While waiting for something cool about them to show,
Then an epic poem about these mighty nuts I can compose.
Because one day something exciting will happen to pistachios.

Summer Smile

You smiled at me in the summer,
I remember the warmth of your look.
Passion it seemed was in bloom,
As my heart you took.

You smiled at me in the autumn,
A look that blew me away.
Part of me seemed to wither,
My heart started to decay.

You smiled at me in the winter,
A harsh look that wouldn't yield.
Your cold snap seized me,
My heart with ice was filled.

You smiled at me in the spring,
A fresh look blossoming on your face.
Our cycle begins again,
My heart refreshed awakes.

Mobile Phone Blues

I used to love to own, a little mobile phone,
But now you see, I don't think it loves me.
As all day it will drone, causing me often to moan,
This ringing persistently, is giving me misery.

Always at it I'm glancing, always it seems I'm answering,
Friend's alleged urgent texts, or whatever comes next.
My phone is always badgering, or for me clamouring,
Constantly it I check, constantly it leaves me vexed.

This phone disturbs my life, and even worse my wifes,
"You're always on the phone," to me she moans.
I fear even in the afterlife, this phone will ruin my life,
But no time to stop I groan, as off again goes my phone.

But I do have a solution, to my phones noise pollution,
It was as easy as ABC, to restore peace and quiet to me.
Yes this phones persecution, had a simple solution.
It has a switch you see, I can turn it off quite simply.

No Brakes

Life can be full of ups and downs,
It's like you're riding a bike,
You strain to pedal to the top of a hill,
Then enjoy the view, what's not to like?

But as you begin your descent something snaps,
You swear you can hear life start to laugh.
As your bike's brakes suddenly fail,
Propelling you straight down the hilly path.

"No brakes, I've got no brakes,"
You shout for help to the sky.
"No brakes, I've got no brakes,"
You scream at passers-by.

Don't panic, let the ride exhilarate you,
Joyfully pedal until you drop.
Who needs brakes anyway?
You shouldn't care that you can't stop.

Because we all really need to ride,
Every now and then without brakes.
So you can experience life to the full,
Yelling out as you make your escape.

"No brakes, I've got no brakes,"
You shout to encourage passers-by.
"No brakes, I've got no brakes,
You should all really give it a try."

The Great Triceratops Robbery

If you're going to steal a life size plastic Triceratops
You're really going to need to pull out all the stops.
Make sure you have a completely cunning plan,
Plus some incredibly drunk friends to hand.

First be certain you can locate the Triceratops,
Plan your route carefully, don't get lost.
Strike quickly in the dark, show no fear,
Then you and the dinosaur can chug a beer.

Down the road you carry your prehistoric pal,
You stagger drunkenly with a celebratory yell.
Pause, savour the moment as best as you can,
Then toast the theft, a drink in both hands.

But the three horned beast is very heavy,
You worry for the prank you're not ready.
You need more help, you've come too far,
Luckily you've stopped outside a bar.

So you leave the poor Triceratops in the street,
While to the pub you beat a hasty retreat.
There a new cunning plan to create,
While the dinosaur patiently awaits its fate.

So outside the pub the Triceratops still stands,
Inspite of all your brilliant drunken plans.
Because you know if the truth be told,
Nothing quite goes right when drink is involved.

But the Triceratops does not judge,
That you abandoned it to go to the pub.
It stands and looks happily at the sky,
New found freedom shining in its plastic eyes.

Regret

I'm sitting in the pub corner,
Comfy in my favourite seat.
Raising my glass half-heartedly,
To all the friends I used to meet.

I'm drinking to your memory,
I'm drinking to regret.
I'm drinking to your health,
I'm drinking to forget.

I wonder if you're close now,
In a room across the road.
Or are your living far away,
On the other side of the globe.

I could see if you are on Facebook,
I could send you a tweet.
Maybe if I looked hard I might
Spot your face in the street.

But no I stay in the pub corner,
Happily nursing my beer.
And if I think I see you passing,
I'll not raise my glass in cheers.

You see I've found I don't miss you,
I really don't give a toss.
That we're no longer friends,
It's my gain and your loss.

So please keep your distance,
Stay away, stay in my past.
Cos I'll stop thinking about you,
When I reach the bottom of my glass.

Light is….

Light is electromagnetic radiation
Each day illuminating the nation.
Lighting up the morning sky,
Burning images onto your eyes.
As the light dawns the morning starts to chorus,
While quickly home the nocturnal rush.
Plants wake and stretch for the sky,
Hungry for the light to survive.
But it's not just above the ground.
That light can be found.
As even at the bottom of the darkest ocean,
Light can cause an illuminating commotion.
As here it shines with eerie bioluminescence,
Like a vampire squid's deadly essence.
Or an angler fish's lurking lure,
Drawing the unwary into its jaws.
But I'm getting ahead what about light's history?
Let's illuminate some of the mystery.
Light like us humans has evolved,
Light like us has a story to be told.
It was firelight that got us started,
Then came gas light which soon departed.
To give way to modern electric light,
Available 24 hours a day to banish night.
But you'll notice folks jump in fright,
If you mention to them nuclear light.
And now we can carry light around,
In our pockets all over town.
From a lighter to a torch,
Or our mobile phone of course.
Light will continue day after day,
And we'd miss it if it went away.
So here's a final thought for you,
We'd like light all the time it's true.
But remember in order for light to shine,
We have to put up with the darkness sometime.

In and Out

I pull a cigarette from the pack,
And pull an idea from the back
Of my mind, but I just don't learn,
As again I let them both burn.

My lighter sparks and warms my hands,
As I remember all my plans.
That never progressed past being lame,
Then died so swiftly like my lighter's flame.

I raise the cigarette to my lips,
Inhaling deeply while my mind slips.
Into input then overload mode,
As I draw in new ideas as I draw in smoke.

Finally I take my last drag,
Stubbing out the remains of my fag.
I find my new ideas I can't remember,
As they die just like my cigarette embers.

Undying Love

I remember our eyes meeting across a graveyard,
Then as we both stopped to pick them up.
Rotting desire gripped our putrid bodies,
We were both stricken with undying love.

I immediately asked you for your hand,
Which I still keep it in an old green pickle jar.
When you asked me for something in return
I was happy to lose my withered heart.

You promised me you'd run away with me,
It started well, until your leg rotted.
So I gave you one of mine to take its place,
I don't mind hopping, I'm besotted.

I said I'd love you until my last breath,
Then I realised my lungs stopped last week.
You said it was the thought that counts,
As you gnawed romantically on my cheek.

I'm sure our undying love will last forever,
We won't part no matter how much we rot.
Because when we finally decompose I've chosen,
To have us both recycled as organic compost.

Waiting for the Bonfire Flames

I'm just a poor old guy on your bonfire,
No firework watching tonight for me.
I'm waiting to be burnt alive,
While you watch and eat your tea.
I'm loaded with your memories,
I wear your granddad's hat.
I sport your dad's old trousers,
My hair's your old bath mat.
But you don't care for this,
You're just here to see me burn.
I fry for your delight tonight,
My fiery demise isn't your concern.
The bonfire starts to flicker,
And then the flames draw closer.
This is your prompt to rave and cheer,
Soon for me it will all be over.
Finally the fire catches,
I'm burning oh so bright.
Joining all the other guys,
On this flaming bonfire night.
And in the morning I'll be ashes,
To be quickly tidied and cleared.
Or scattered gently by the wind,
Until I'm resurrected next year

The Useless Ghost

So here I am haunting the corner of your living room,
With a tatty white sheet over my head.
Pondering what it means to be a ghost,
Now that you've got your wish and I'm dead.

I ask myself why I need a sheet,
It doesn't scare me so I'm sure it won't you.
But I presume all ghosts must wear one,
When they jump out and say boo.

What's with this saying boo anyway?
Would it really make you jump in fright?
To be honest I've eaten curries,
That have given me scarier nights.

I want to know why I'm haunting you?
As alive I was better at making you scream.
But now I'm a sheet wearing ghost,
I don't scare you at all it seems.

Do we have unfinished business?
Is that why I'm haunting you, we discuss.
To be honest I think we're both embarrassed,
That even my death hasn't separated us.

To annoy me you start to date an exorcist,
So I've decided to put up no resistance.
If you ask him to banish me I'll go quietly,
Happy to leave you and my dreary after life existence.

Urban Child

In an unremarkable street
There was a complicated birth.
Leaving an urban child
Lying tense and twisted
Unfit for this straight world.
Fists clenched, he's a fighter
Who sleeps fitfully.

The child becomes a boy
One who always takes
The long route to school.
Geometry teaches him
How some shapes don't fit in
No matter how much you bend
Or try to force them.

The boy becomes a teen
One who knows all the shortcuts
To all the pubs.
Who sits wedged in their corners
White knuckles clenched
Round a pint,
While emotions froth.

Finally the teen becomes a man.
Who chain smokes tensely
As his child joins the world.
Another ill-fitting specimen.
He holds them tight
Then whispers,
"Never change, it will all be fine."

Thoughts on Modern Love

Our eyes certainly never met over a cliché
Though I did detect a twinkle when we exchanged glances.
No rom-com spark of electricity was generated
We just swapped shy smiles and quiet chat.
A string quartet didn't strike up as you entered the room
Though we did lend each other our favourite CD's.
I never had a comic misunderstanding with your parents
Instead we just had a nice cup of tea.
Your ex didn't suddenly appear back in your life
However we did laugh about our past mistakes.
We never drove off into the sunset
As your Mini was in for an MOT.
This was never a Hollywood romance,
Yet I still got the girl and the happy ending.

Outside Looking In

We're all on the outside looking in,
Breathing on the windows,
Rubbing them with grimy sleeves.
We want to know what we're missing,
Our insatiable curiosity
Blocked by grimy glass.
We swear we can hear voices,
Is that a party going on?
Why weren't we invited?

We're all on the outside looking in,
Getting desperate to find out,
Just exactly what's inside.
Our bodies press forwards,
Surging and jostling,
Eager to discover what we're missing.
Is it the proverbial Promised Land?
Where everything is better than what we have now.
And no one is ever alone.

We're still on the outside looking in,
Determined to find out,
Why we were left out in the cold.
Then a common thought occurs,
That slowly germinates into an idea,
How could we be so stupid?
If we are all outside
Then who is inside
And going to let us in?

Is Friday the Thirteenth Unlucky?

Should a nation quake in fear,
As it's Friday the thirteenth today?
Should I worry about bad luck,
Wish this day would go away?
Who chose Friday the thirteenth anyway,
Why is this day such bad news?
Well we need to go back in history,
To see why this day gives us the blues.
Supposedly many many years ago,
Eve in Eden on this fateful Friday.
Chomped on an apple and caused the curse,
When she was only eating one of her five a day.
Now you can't go out for lunch,
If there's another twelve going, but still
This might only be unlucky,
If you're landed with the bill.
Thirteen has a lot of bad press,
Unlike its close friend twelve.
As we're happy with twelve months,
And that a clock has twelve hours.
But just add one and we're on the edge,
That little addition makes us stop.
Thirteen can cause heart attacks,
Make us think we're for the chop.
How badly are we affected by thirteen?
Well just think on this.
How many buildings are there,
Where thirteen doesn't exist.
They have no thirteenth floor,
There might not be a ward thirteen.
There's no thirteenth room,
Lifts go straight from twelve to fourteen.
Should I care about this?
With this bad karma am I stuck?
I'll tell you all tomorrow on Saturday
When I should have better luck.

Unfathomable

In a quiet corner of the park,
Lies a lake with water dark.
Surrounded by stooped trees.
Which guard it from the breeze.

If at its shores you stand there,
It seems no matter how long you stare.
The lake's depths defy your gaze,
Whether you look for minutes or days.

But be patient, stand very still,
Put away your phone, wait until.
Very slowly before your eyes,
The lake quietly comes to life.

The surface ripples, then breaks,
As a water boatman skates.
Then a branch shakes and sways,
As a squirrel makes his way.

But as soon as nature comes it goes,
Your spectacle draws to a close.
Nature again hides away,
To perhaps return another day.

The trees seem to close ranks,
As you steal a final glance.
Then the lake's water fades to black,
As you turn and don't look back.

Little Vlad

Not many people know that,
When Dracula was young he had a pet.
A small furry vampire gerbil,
Who wore a little black cape and vest.
Little Vlad the gerbil's name was,
He was the terror of Dracula's garden.
Even though at first glance he looked cute,
Very quickly your heart would harden.
As you saw Little Vlad teasing snakes,
Or picking a fight with some wolves.
He might hide in trees and bite bats,
Or catch fish with his teeth by the pool.
All the other animals in the garden,
Decided they'd had enough.
Little Vlad they said was a total pest,
But who would stand up to a gerbil so tough?
The up stepped Professor Rabbit,
Who said he had a marvellous idea.
And how in the space of one week,
Little Vlad from the garden he'd clear.
But there would be a price to pay,
If the animals would be rid of Little Vlad.
Professor Rabbit requested,
Any spare body parts they had.
So Fox bravely sacrificed his tail,
Badger cut off a paw.
Owl donated a wing,
And Raven gave a claw.
The Professor Rabbit set to work,
He gathered up all the parts.
And set to work in his lab,
His mysterious project to start.
To all the animal bits,
He added parts from fresh graves.
With eyes and teeth from jars,
Plus other organs he had saved.

Then a week later,
As a thunder storm filled the sky.
Professor Rabbit pulled a switch,
And bought his creation to life.
That day Little Vlad was in the garden,
Doing his usual stalking around.
When he nearly jumped out of his fur,
When he heard a blood curdling sound.
Lumbering and roaring a monster came,
Made from animal bits sewn tight.
The animals wondered would Little Vlad flee
Or would there be a fight?
Little Vlad looked the monster up and down,
Something about it caught his eye.
What on earth was about to happen?
Then Little Vlad began to sigh.
It seems Professor Rabbit's monster
Had stolen his little heart
The monstrosity at Vlad tried to roar
Then it stopped with a start
As Little Vlad dropped to one knee,
And held up one of his paws.
Then he swore eternal love,
To the fellow fiend that he saw.
The monster tried to speak,
But its poorly sewn tongue fell out.
So to declare its love for Little Vlad,
It uttered a blood curdling shout.
So now the animals limp around,
Their garden is quiet and serene.
Loss of limbs was worth it,
To be rid of Little Vlad the fiend.
And everywhere there is peace,
Contentment reigns on the garden slopes.
As Little Vlad the little charmer,
With Franken bunny has eloped.

Cat vs. Christmas Tree

I flick my tail at your Christmas decorations,
I raise my hackles at your holly and all that.
I curl my lip at your Christmas cards,
This season there's only one mission for this cat.

And that is in my role as feline predator,
I'm going to stealthily stalk your Christmas tree.
My mission is simply to kill it you know,
Oh just you wait and see.

I raise a paw and unsheathe my claws,
I prepare the killing blow.
I strike as quick as lightning,
Down the Christmas tree goes.

Oh bugger I'm trapped beneath it now,
With a tree light illuminating my arse.
I hiss, spit and caterwaul,
But my plight gets worse because.

In runs my owner, all red in the face,
"You wretched animal, "he shouts out loud.
Trying his best to find me,
As under the tree's remains I cower.

"I'll skin you cat you tree wrecker you,"
My owner says as he brandishes a knife.
He's over reacting a little I think,
I'm sure he won't take one of my nine lives.

As my owner lifts what's left of the tree,
I spot an open door and leg it outside.
Leaving him to tidy up the mess,
With lots of swearing and sighs.

Later I peer through the lounge window,
Looking like butter wouldn't melt in my mouth.
I'll be back for that tree tomorrow,
And the turkey better look out as well.

Winter Coat

In the cupboard all summer you've waited,
Next to bags of Christmas wrapping paper.
Your collar still all frayed and worn,
Your pockets with the lining still torn.
Patiently waiting for your time to come,
Quietly waiting for the Autumn.
To be taken down and dusted off
To protect the wearer from wind and frost.
Then once the weather has fully recovered,
Never complain as you return to the cupboard.

The Man who Death Forgot

This is the story of the man who Death forgot.
A man who lived his life in such an inconsequential way
That he slipped between the cracks of existence.
So that when it came time for the man to die
Death just overlooked him, then forgot all about him.
Now the man continues with his grey life
A life so devoid of feeling and colour
That even his rainbows are black and white.
Now he waits patiently
But for what he's not sure.

This is the story of the man who Death forgot.
Who often sits in silence
Watching time ebb slowly around him
While he remains untouched by its waves
As they smash against the cliffs of reality
Slowly crumbling the world pebble by pebble
Until nothing remains
As the man watches
Finding despite his jealously
He finds he cannot turn his eyes away.

This is the story of the man who Death forgot.
Whose eyes are drawn towards a silent forest.
A forest he remembers planting as acorns
Then tenderly walking among the growing saplings
Caring for them until
They became mighty oaks whose branches challenge the sky.
The man's critical gaze spots the first trace of decay
He knows the forest will fall
Then the mighty oaks will be left to lie and rot
While life moves on without him.

This is the story of the man who Death forgot.
Who has outlived everyone he ever knew
But still hopes that one day
He will feel a hand touch his shoulder.
Then he prays he will be released from his half-life
So that the time's touch will wash him clean
And that the forest will outlast him
The cliffs will still stand
Until he finally becomes
The man who Death remembered.

The Shop of Lost Poems

Have you ever woken from a dream,
With a poem vanishing from your sight.
And as you struggle to remember it,
It fades, along with the night.

Or have you ever been on the bus,
And felt a poem creep up on you.
But had no pen or paper ready,
So the poem just fell through.

Do you ever stop to think,
Where do your lost poems go?
They don't just fade and vanish,
They have a home you know.

Somewhere in a dark street,
In a long forgotten part of town.
Stands a small crooked shop,
All battered and run down.

On its dusty shelves,
Are found lost poems and ideas.
Sprawled in disorganised piles,
Gathered over the years.

How the poems got there is uncertain,
Why they come here none can explain.
All that's known is here's their home,
As they wait to be found again.

Now say you stumble on this shop,
Finding a poem you thought lost.
You wish to buy it back,
You're willing to pay the cost.

The charge on a sign reads,
If you want back a poem never spoken.
Then the price is simple,
We charge a poem for a poem.

Be careful before you pay though,
Make sure you're willing to give up.
That thing you cherish the most
A poem you've written and love?

You might think the deal worth it,
But beware on leaving the shop.
You may find your returned poem,
Is once again easily forgot.

The shop offers no refunds,
It doesn't allow you to return.
So perhaps here's a lesson,
That we all could learn.

Cherish your new poems and ideas,
Don't chase those you lost and regret.
Just enjoy and continue with,
Whatever poem you think of next.

Exercising my Demons

Today I'm exercising my demons,
I hope I've not left it too late.
They're complaining and screaming
But they're so unfit and overweight.

Yes I'm going to get my demons fit,
On the treadmill they can go.
They're getting better bit by bit
But there's a problem now you know.

You see once I'd let my demons out,
They didn't want to go back.
They scream loudly and they shout,
Discretion they sadly lack.

So now I've exercised all my demons,
They're up to no good running about.
Better to have unhealthy demons it seems
Than think you can fix them by letting them out.

Kam 4 Tony B 4 Eva

Kam 4 Tony B 4 eva
Sprayed on an underpass wall.
Love so boldly declared,
With a vandal's scrawl.

Kam 4 Tony B 4 eva,
Does either of them know.
Of this spray painted statement,
That has put their love on show.

Kam 4 Tony B 4 eva,
Will people cry?
If they separate
Before the paint is dry.

School Daze

Holes in tights and love bites,
Every lunchtime a playground fights.
School rules and class fools,
Inappropriate use of woodwork tools.
Dirty socks and high frocks,
Biology lessons causing shocks.
Stolen bikes and teacher's strikes,
Cancelled after school hikes.
Borrowing LP's and bruised knees,
After class "please see me."
Inattention and detention,
Cheeking teachers means suspension.
Are these the best days of your life?
Or just a different type of strife?

An Open Letter to the Fox in my Road

Dear Mr Fox I'm writing directly to you,
As I want to set a few things straight.
Folk in my street may think you're cute,
But I don't think you're that great.
Your mangy tail and flea ridden coat,
Somehow endears you to my neighbours.
But please stop digging up my lawn,
And chewing on my newspapers.
Then when you visit my garden,
Just try to be more clean.
There's plenty of bushes and plants,
So why crap on our trampoline?
You know our dustbin holds only rubbish,
Not some hidden fox snack or treat.
So why do you knock it over,
Spilling the contents down the street.
I want you to be aware Mr Fox,
That when you next make your rounds.
If I see any more of your bad ways,
I'm going to release the hounds.

Remember/Forget

We can all forget things it's true,
Trivial thoughts can easily slip our mind,
Phones or keys can be misplaced,
Sometimes you lose track of the time.
But what if you forgot something,
That was a large chunk of your life?
What if you lost those thoughts forever?
Like you forgot you had children or a wife.
What if these lost memories teased you,
Flitting back briefly into your brain.
Only to vanish again just as quick,
While at your failing memory you complain.
What if your family and friends tried to help,
Doing their best to get through to you.
Powerless though to help you remember,
Looking on, hiding tears at what you forget to do.
Think on this next time you can't remember,
Something trivial you were going to do.
Your memories will return, then when they do,
Remember those who can't remember you.

Cold on the Bus

It's cold on the bus this morning,
Frost coats the inside of the window.
Making my morning commute,
A chilly mystery tour.
Cold breath escapes mouths,
Rising slovenly into the air.
As hands huddle in pockets
While collars are all turned up.
I scratch at the glass,
Wondering where we are.
Cars shoot by, cosy wombs of warmth,
Sparking jealously as I shiver.
My iPod plays summer songs,
Fake warmth into my ears
While my toes cringe
As winter bites hard.
I contemplate getting my pen out
To commit the cold to paper
Thinking better of it
My hands remain in my pocket's toasty nests.
Cold doesn't inspire, or does it?
I wonder does nature's chill not slow synapses
But instead produce
A hot spark of creativity?
Surely without the inspiration of cold,
We'd never have discovered fire?
Lucky ancestors I think
As I wonder when I'll arrive and feel warm again.

Saga Louts

We are the grey haired army,
Abroad and on the lash again.
Walking sticks and lager ready,
We wobble off ships and planes.

We've got our kids inheritance,
We've cashed in our pensions.
We're getting obscene tattoos,
In places you shouldn't mention.

Hopping in and out of hotel beds,
Laughing as we trash cruise ships.
Playing naked oily Twister,
Despite our dodgy arthritic hips.

Bill has only got one kidney,
Doris has a new glass eye.
But there's no stopping us,
If cheap sangria we spy.

We'll riot as we drink the lot,
Pogo dance all through the night.
Shovel down kebab and chips,
Throw up, then have a fight.

Then when the holiday's over,
We stagger home a little slower.
Our only holiday souvenirs,
A sunburn and hangover.

Darkness

The Darkness sneers,
It's black tongue licks tombstone teeth,
While entropy dribbles from
Lips that smack together like a corpse lands on a slab.
The light is its prey tonight.

The Darkness flows around vehicles,
Slavering over their red and yellow lights,
Allowing them one last wink,
Before gorging on their brightness.
Leaving their owners stranded in the gloom.

The Darkness gnaws on street lights
Lapping up their circles of light,
Cracking bulbs like a dog cracks a bone.
Leaving concrete frames,
Bent like groping old blind men.

The Darkness silently spreads,
Like an insidious bacterial culture.
Festering and multiplying.
A cancer of the light,
A terminal case.

Chuggers

With your t-shirt just so rightly tight,
It's logo conveniently at chest height,
You approach me with a flirty smile,
I become instantly the beguiled.
Apparently you are collecting for charity,
Not that your words to me have clarity,
I bet you collect more than the guys,
I think as I drown into your eyes.
So I don't notice signing the direct debit,
Though on payday I will regret it,
But it was worth it for our brief chat,
And hours of pleasant thoughts after that.

Dinner for One

Dinner for one I think again,
My evenings are always the same.
As half-heartedly I browse shelves,
Wondering what to cook for myself.

Lonely I suppose you might call me,
As I eat in the pale glow of my TV.
Thinking on friendships that died,
Because I never really tried.

Now I call ready meals my friend,
As unlike people they don't pretend.
To be anything but what you see,
That's why I prefer their company.

I finish my meal then take my pills,
Not certain if they contain my ills.
As I wash them down I always try,
To supress my pain before I cry.

I sit silently in a daze as people call,
Doctors or Nurses I've seen them all.
Bandaging my loneliness with meds,
Unable to fix what's wrong in my head.

Before I try to sleep I online shop,
For oven chips, a solitary pork chop.
I almost forgot, just one thing more,
As I click quickly on wine for four.

Child in a Rose Garden

A wall of vibrant colour
Momentarily,
Stops my daughter in her steps.
Then keen to explore,
She quickly approaches
The garden's centrepiece.
Recognition hits,
Like sunbeams
Strike petals.
Her face lights up
Mirroring the roses' bloom.
A smile dawns.

Hands reach out
Knowing not to touch,
But doing so anyway.
Blue eyes widen
Slowly a tongue,
Becomes untied.
"I like your roses Daddy,
But these are prettier."

My Burial Arrangements

Don’t bury me where bells chime,
Don’t bury me where phones beep.
Don’t bury me where poets rhyme,
I don’t want a disturbed sleep.

Don’t bury me on the ocean bed,
Don’t bury me where crabs creep.
Don’t bury me with the watery dead,
I don’t want to be fish food as I sleep.

Don’t bury me where warriors lie,
Don’t bury me where widows weep.
Don’t bury me where children cry,
I don’t deserve a heroes sleep.

I Love You More

I love you more than the smell of freshly baked bread,
I love you more than waking up and finding I'm not dead.
I love you more than coming home drunk,
I love you more than eating the last chocolate chunk.
I love you more than the first cigarette of the day,
I love you more than my wages being paid.
I love you more than a doughnut's sugar on my lips,
I love you more than a dolphin's kiss.
I love you more than all the new books on my shelf,
I love you more than life itself.

Newsflash

The other day I saw a curious sight,
A man in the street reading a book.
I had to stop and rub my eyes,
Then take another look.

But I wasn't having a hallucination
A man was reading the printed page.
He wasn't using an iPhone or Kindle,
Doesn't he know they're all the rage?

As I watched cars and buses stopped,
People gave the man three cheers.
"Hooray he's reading from a book,
We'd heard they'd disappeared."

T.V crews quickly turned up
Plus radio broadcasters too.
There's a man reading an actual book,
Soon became the headline news.

Despite all this the book reading man,
Made no effort to stop or look.
He didn't notice the fuss he'd caused,
It must have been a hell of a book.

Afterword

There you go I've said my piece,
I've given my words release.
Set them free on the wind,
Wondering where they will land.

Did you listen or not to them?
Where you moved when
I stood up and spoke?
Or did you think me just a joke?

Anyway I don't care now.
My words have been released so.
They'll find a home somewhere,
The exact place I don't care.

ENJOYED THE BOOK AND WANT TO READ MORE OF MY POETRY?

Then why not join me on my poetry blog – "Poems and More from Richard Archer."

My blog has been running now for over five years, it's a place where I post my new poems, news of what I'm up to and more several times a week.

On the site you can read all my poetry old and new, watch videos of me reciting my works live or from my TV appearances, enjoy poetry from special guests and more all for free.

It's easy to find just type the blogs title into Google and up it will pop. If you like what you read you can subscribe to the blog and every time I post a new article or poem you will get an email – no spam I promise.

There's more PTO for details of my other book.

ALSO BY RICHARD ARCHER:

"BEER FROTH" – A POETRY COLLECTION.

AVAILABLE AS A BOOK ON LULU OR FOR KINDLE ON AMAZON

Beer Froth is a collection of poetry from Walsall poet Richard Archer. The book is a selection of poetry from his successful poetry blog and new work written especially for this collection.

Richard's poetry is a mix of what he observes in his daily commute and whatever is in his head when he the urge to write overtakes him. His poem "OCP" explains why he will never stop writing, whereas "Marmite Covered Jelly Babies" shows just how difficult it can be to understand the opposite sex. From Were Hamsters and office ghosts to seagulls and take away kebabs, this is a collection designed to hopefully make you laugh and think. Not necessarily in that order.

Praise for Beer Froth

"After reading this joyous romp of vampires, cake and just about everything in between, I was left with a huge grin on my face. The writer though is far from just a poet of comical rhyme. He has a skill in his craft that is often quite insightful. I find the observational poetry of daily commutes both real and accurate in their descriptive content. Overall a great read and I would thoroughly recommend this anthology to anyone wishing to pick up a great book of poetry."

"Very enjoyable. Gives a witty insight into the writer's mind. Worth a read, and will likely pick it up again for a giggle! Good stuff."

"In turn funny, poignant and all stops in-between. Highly recommended."

IF YOU ENJOYED THE COVER THEN WHY NOT MEET THE PHOTOGRAPHER AND DESIGNER:

ANDY SIMON FROM DARKSLIDE PHOTOGRAPHY

Andy is an award winning, internationally published Photographer, Film Maker, Graphic Designer and Educator from the West Midlands, holding a Licentiateship with the British Institute of Professional Photography in recognition of his work in the industry, as well as a Batchelor of Arts Degree in Visual Communication with Honours.

Passionate about breaking the norms of society on how people perceive beauty, Andy specializes in alternative and creative high fashion concepts, and has worked with many performers and models within the industry. He often works on large scale productions, utilizing a strong team of models, fashion designers, stylists and makeup artists to create intricately detailed images and art work, with a particular emphasis towards more fantasy and fairy tale styles, blending photography with digital artwork. Most recently he has written and directed his first short movie "Jessica's Doll" In which the author of this book wrote the introductionary poem for.

Andy can be found on Facebook on his page Darkslide photography or his website which bears the same name.

#0237 - 120916 - C0 - 210/148/6 - PB - DID1580119